Jack's Library

by Tirrell Anthony

Illustrated by Lane Gregory

PEARSON

Glenview, Illinois • Boston, Massachusetts • Chandler, Arizona
Upper Saddle River, New Jersey

What can you do with a room like Jack's?
He has books in piles and books in packs.
Jack likes to read a book each day.
And he never puts a book away.
And when he goes to bed at night,
He reads more books with a flashlight.

Books scattered here, books scattered there,
Jack could not even find his chair.
"This must stop," his mother said.
Clean up those books, and get to bed!"

"Clean them up? What can I do?
I don't know where to start; that is true.
Should I hide my collection under my bed?
Or should I take it outside to the shed?"

---

shed: small building used for storage

stack

The first idea tried by Jack
Was to put the books in one big stack.
He made a stack right on the floor.
He pushed the stack behind the door.
"Now how can I find a book in here?
I did not think of that, it's clear."

"Wait a minute! What is this I see?
A book called How to Make a Library!
I will read this book. I'll get it right."
And so he read for half the night.
Finally, Jack's plan was set.
"I'll arrange them like the alphabet!"

---

arrange: put in order

"I'll stack the books that start with A,
Then make a B stack, right away.
Then a stack for C, then D, then E.
That is how it's going to be."
Jack sorted books from A to Z.
He organized them happily.

---

organized: put into groups

Jack's mother saw them on the shelf.
She asked: "Did you do this all yourself?"
"I had a plan," said Jack with pride.
"The library is open. Come inside!"

---

pride: feeling good about what you did